Ethics of Food

Making Food Choices

Michael Burgan

Heinemann Library
Chicago, Illinois

Edited by Adam Miller, Andrew Farrow, and Adrian
Vigliano
Designed by Ryan Frieson
Illustrated by Mapping Specialists, Ltd. and
Planman Technologies
Picture research by Tracy Cummins
Originated by Capstone Global Library Ltd.
Printed and bound in the United States of America
by Corporate Graphics in North Mankato,
Minnesota
15 14 13 12 11
10 9 8 7 6 5 4 3 2 1

**Library of Congress Cataloging-in-Publication
Data**
Cataloging-in-Publication data is on file at the
Library of Congress.

ISBN 978-1-4329-5104-7 (HB)
ISBN 978-1-4329-6194-7 (PB)

Acknowledgements

The author and publisher are grateful to the
following for permission to reproduce copyright
material: Alamy p. 9 (© Frances Roberts); AP
Photo pp. 34 (Mike Stewart), 48 (Reed Saxon);
Corbis pp. 41 (© AgStock Images), 47 (© Peter
Dench/In Pictures); Defenseimagery.mil p. 11
(U.S. Army photo by Sgt. Jason Bushong); Getty
Images pp. 13 (Luciana Whitaker/LatinContent),
20 (AFP PHOTO/ Tiziana Fabi), 29 (Beth Hall/
Bloomberg), 30 (Dan Kitwood), 31 (Fabrizio
Constantini/Bloomberg), 36 (MICHAEL MATHES/
AFP); istockphoto pp. 26 (© Francisco Orellana),
43 (© graphixel); Shutterstock pp. 5 (© Jonathan
Feinstein), 7 (© Richard Thornton), 15 (© thumb),
16 (© ppart), 19 (© Melinda Fawver), 23 (©
Picsfive), 25 (© Artur Bogacki), 33 (© Tommaso
Lizzul), 39 (© Christian Lagerek), 46 (© Kang
Khoon Seang).

Cover photograph of a shopping cart with food
in reproduced with permission of Getty Images
(Roderick Chen).

We would like to thank Christopher Nicolson for
his invaluable help in the preparation of this book.

Every effort has been made to contact copyright
holders of any material reproduced in this book.
Any omissions will be rectified in subsequent
printings if notice is given to the publisher.

All the Internet addresses (URLs) given in this book
were valid at the time of going to press. However,
due to the dynamic nature of the Internet, some
addresses may have changed, or sites may have
changed or ceased to exist since publication. While
the author and publisher regret any inconvenience
this may cause readers, no responsibility for any
such changes can be accepted by either the author
or the publisher.

Contents

Some words are printed in bold, **like this**. You can find out what they mean by looking in the glossary.

Choosing Your Food

For millions of the world's people, eating their daily food is a simple act, one they might do without much thought. Their toughest choices might be where they will eat (at home or in a restaurant) and what will be on the menu (beef, fish, or maybe pasta). But behind those decisions are much tougher ones, called **ethical** decisions. These are decisions people make based on their values, meaning their sense of what is right and wrong.

Food ethics

What are some of the ethical issues raised by food? One is: What is the best way to grow the most affordable, nutritious food—without damaging the world we live in? Another issue looks at the business of food. Is our demand for cheap and convenient food forcing some workers and farmers to accept wages and prices so low that they barely have enough money to live on? Other issues involve choosing the best foods to eat—foods that provide plenty of nutrition, without adding to **pollution** or other environmental problems.

People around the globe are asking these and similar questions every day. They face the moral rights and wrongs surrounding the production, sale, and consumption of food. And beyond some of the more detailed questions, people confront one larger one. Even in the world's wealthiest and healthiest countries, people still go hungry, or they eat too much food with little nutritional value. And the problem is worse in poorer nations. So, how can the world work together to solve this issue? Can it be solved?

As you read this book, think about the ethics of food. What choices can people make to try to provide enough food to everyone, while preserving their health—as well as treating the planet in a sustainable way?

Walk through the aisles of your local supermarket and you will see shelves packed with a wide variety of packaged foods. The produce section is filled with fruits and vegetables of all sizes and colors, grown all over the world. In wealthy nations, a large supermarket may carry more than 40,000 different food and beverage products. That is a lot of choices.

What influences which foods you and other people buy? What forces shape which foods farmers grow and how they grow them? Taking a box of cereal off the shelf and going to the cash register seems like a simple act. But before you make that choice, a lot of effort and a lot of money have gone into producing that food—and then convincing you to buy it.

Modern supermarkets offer shoppers tens of thousands of choices—but in most poor countries, choices are more limited.

The importance of food

From an early age, we learn the importance of food. It gives us the energy we need to live. It provides the **nutrients** we need to be healthy. But food is more than just something we take in to keep our minds and bodies strong. Throughout history, humans have placed great importance on how they get their food and how they eat it.

The ease of buying tonight's meal at a neighborhood store might make us forget that our ancestors had a much harder time getting food. In ancient times, hunting for wild animals was a crucial act of survival for an entire community. Teaching young people how to hunt and prepare food was perhaps the most important part of their education. Gathering wild crops was also part of this education. In some remote parts of the world, hunting, gathering, and simple farming are still the main sources of daily meals.

Over time, meals also became a focus of celebrations and important events. Sharing food with others was a way to show friendship, respect, and love. The English word "companionship" shows the link between food and personal relationships. It traces its roots to the Latin words "*com*" and "*panis*," meaning "with bread." Our companions are the people we sit with at a dinner table, enjoying food.

The big business of food

Today, the making and selling of food is a huge business, providing jobs for millions of people around the world. Large international companies often control what food is sold and how it is produced. "**Agribusiness**" refers to the production of products related to farming and food production on a large scale, with goods that are often sold around the world. One part of this is so-called **factory farms**, where thousands of animals are raised quickly so they can be used for food. The **industrialized** production of food—both livestock and crops—has led, for the most part, to lower food costs and the almost unlimited choices you see in the store.

Food choices—at a cost?

As we will see, the rise of agribusiness has not solved all the problems related to food. Some people still go hungry. And some people do not have easy access to nutritious, affordable food. The production of large quantities of certain foods also poses potential problems to the environment. These include damage to the water supply from chemicals used in **agriculture**, damage to the soil, and the production of gases that lead to the rise in average temperatures known as **global warming**.

Industrial machines, such as this one that washes carrots, have made it much faster and easier to produce food products.

The world's top five retailers that sell food		
Company	Headquarters	Sales in billions of U.S. dollars (2008)
Wal-Mart	United States	405.6
Carrefour S.A.	France	129.8
Metro AG	Germany	99.9
Tesco plc	United Kingdom	96.2
Schwarz Unternehmen	Germany	79.9

This chart shows the world's five largest sellers of food.

Problems of the Western diet

Even for those people with easy access to food, the food itself sometimes poses problems to **consumers**. For more than 70 years, researchers have talked about the "Western diet" (see pages 14 and 15). This diet is made up of the foods commonly eaten in North America, Europe, Australia, and other wealthy, industrialized nations. This diet is usually heavy on **refined** grains (which means that the grains have lower proportions of many nutrients than the unrefined grain), sugar, meat, and dairy. It often has few vegetables and fruits and is high in salt and fat. Whenever the Western diet is introduced into new parts of the world, scientists see a rise in certain diseases, particularly type 2 **diabetes**, heart disease, and certain cancers.

How can people avoid the dangers of the Western diet? The answer would seem to be simple. They can choose healthier foods. But foods containing sugar, fat, and refined grains are common products of agribusiness. They are produced in huge quantities, and their prices tend to be low. And agribusiness companies spend millions of dollars each year convincing shoppers to buy certain foods—some of which are products that have very little nutritional value.

Food security

The concept of providing everyone with adequate supplies of affordable, healthy food is sometimes called **food security**. People who tackle this issue see food security as a social and political issue.

Food security is not just about setting up a charity to give packaged foods to the poor. Food security also involves looking at how food is produced, as well as doing what is best for both the environment and society as a whole. Promoters of food security stress the need for **sustainable** food, meaning food that can continue to be produced without hurting the environment. This means supporting locally grown food as much as possible.

In parts of the Western world, one food security issue is the rise of food "deserts." These are areas in cities where residents, usually poor, do not have access to supermarkets. Many large companies do not want to build stores in poor neighborhoods, and the people in those areas often do not have cars. They often end up shopping at small corner markets with overpriced packaged foods and few fresh fruits and vegetables.

In an example from the United States, research from 2009 showed that just over 20 percent of the 2.8 million people in Chicago, Illinois, lived in food deserts. Chicago is the third-largest city in the United States. Researcher Mari Gallagher said about the problem, "You can't choose a healthy diet if you don't have access to it. Many in the food desert who suffer are children who already have diabetes but who have yet to be diagnosed and treated."

Officials in Chicago and other cities work with food security groups to try to convince supermarkets to open in food deserts. Aldi, based in Germany, did open several new stores in Chicago. It offers fewer choices than a typical supermarket, but more than a corner market—and at lower prices.

COLD BEER & SODAS · HOT & COLD SANDWIC

A small store like this might be the only easily accessible source of groceries for some people. It might be hard for those people to reach larger, better-stocked supermarkets.

Sustainable agriculture

In many areas of the world, farmers are rejecting the agribusiness model and returning to older methods of farming, which do not rely on chemicals to control weeds and pests or to provide nutrients to the soil. This type of agriculture is called **organic** farming. It is part of a larger movement called sustainable agriculture. The idea is to sustain, or preserve, the environment and improve people's health while providing enough nutritious food to feed the world.

As we will see, sustainable agriculture gives consumers another set of food choices. The movement stresses buying goods from local farmers, who often raise a variety of crops, dairy, and meat products not found in supermarkets. But prices at farms and farmers' markets are often higher than prices for agribusiness-produced foods at supermarkets—which are often much less nutritious.

Problems with sustainable agriculture

Why is there such a variation in price? Governments give money, called **subsidies**, to many large farmers. This helps reduce the cost of certain farm goods, especially grains and dairy products. These foods are generally **processed** and then made into many packaged and "fast" food options. Subsidized grains are also fed to many animals raised at large factory farms that produce meat, dairy products, and eggs.

In contrast, smaller farmers receive little or no subsidies to grow a variety of crops that are part of a nutritious diet, such as fruits and vegetables. Without subsidies, prices for these foods may be higher than those of processed foods. And livestock raised naturally on these farms will produce more costly food products, such as milk and eggs, as well—although they are often more healthy.

Another problem with sustainable agriculture is that some scientists and most agribusiness officials believe organic farming cannot provide enough food to feed the world, and that, instead, chemicals are necessary to grow all the crops the world needs.

What do you think?

Would it be better to spend more money to help small farms grow sustainable crops, even if that meant less money for the large-scale production of other important crops?

Wars and natural disasters can affect the food supply. Here, people in a war zone receive food from the United Nations.

Yet a 2009 report found that with some small changes in meat and dairy consumption, the world's farmers would be able to sustainably feed everyone on the planet. Choices consumers make in the years to come will influence that outcome.

Fewer choices

For some people, food choices are limited. In poor countries, many people do not have access to a wide range of foods. They eat what they can afford and what is readily available. In some cases, the locally produced food cannot meet all their dietary needs.

According to the United Nations (UN), a lack of proper nutrition kills 3.5 million children worldwide each year. The UN also says there is enough food in the world to end hunger. Several factors, however, affect how the food is distributed. Natural disasters such as **drought** (lack of rainfall) can wipe out crops in one region. Wars sometimes prevent food from reaching the hungry. Poor nations lack the resources to develop their own agriculture. And farming methods, such as cutting forests and using chemicals, reduce the ability of crops to grow on some farmlands.

The food available around the world, or in your local supermarket, is part of a huge food system. Humans and the environment interact to produce food. Political and economic decisions play a part. So do more personal choices—the ones we make every day about what we eat.

All Types of Diets

Counting calories, saying no to certain foods, eating lots of other types of foods—these activities are common for people trying to lose weight. People call their special meal plans a diet, but the word also has a more general meaning. A diet is also the range of foods a person or a group of people typically eat on a day-to-day basis.

For example, for native peoples living along the Arctic Circle, their diet is heavy with fish, seal, and wild game. Across the Western world, the typical diet includes a wide range of grains, meat, fish, dairy products, and fruits and vegetables. And in many parts of Asia, the traditional diet is based around rice, fresh vegetables, and small amounts of meat.

Dietary choices were once limited by the climate and what local soil might be capable of growing. Two hundred years ago, people ate largely what could be raised close to where they lived. For example, centuries ago, someone in Scandinavia would not have been able to squeeze fresh orange juice, since oranges and other citrus fruits only grow in warm climates.

But advances in transportation and refrigeration made it possible for the traditional local-based diet to expand. And the spread of industry around the world, and the rising wages it stirred, meant people had more money to spend on food. At the same time, the cost of buying many foods, such as grains and meat, fell. As a result, the Western diet spread to all but the most remote parts of the world, especially among **urban** (city) populations with good wages.

The spread of technology and wealth gave people the power to choose from a variety of diets. They could opt for foods that they believed made them healthier, or that followed the beliefs of their religion. They could also choose foods they liked and that were produced in ways that did not harm the planet.

The Western diet

Since the rise of modern farming in the 18th century, Western nations have increasingly grown large amounts of certain crops, especially grains. These nations include the wealthiest countries of Europe and South America, as well as the United States, Canada, and Australia. Soybeans are a more recent addition to the list of common Western food crops.

The Inupiat of Alaska still hunt and eat whales, as do other native peoples along the Arctic Circle.

Case study:
A blend of past and present

The native people of Canada are known as the First Nations, and many of them are eager to preserve the eating habits of the past. Since 2007 some tribes on Vancouver Island, in British Columbia, have met at events called Feasting for Change. The feasts are part of an effort to find, cook, and prepare food as their ancestors did.

Seafood, such as halibut and salmon, are a key part of their diet. At the feasts, much of the food is cooked over hot coals in pits, just as in the past.

The feasts are part of a larger movement called food **sovereignty**. This involves giving the First Nations and other local peoples in countries settled by Europeans more rights regarding food. The people want to control the food resources of the region, rather than having private companies own and process the resources. The native people stress the sacred connection they feel to the land and water, and the foods that come from them.

Some of these crops are turned into food products, while some go to feed animals, which provide **protein** through their meat and milk.

The grains used in human food were once whole grains, which contained all the nutrients available. Over time, however, most grains were refined. Refined grains last longer on the shelf and are easier to digest. But the refining process strips them of many of their nutrients. Typical refined grains are white rice sold by the box or white pasta products. Whole-grain foods include brown rice and breads made with whole grains, such as wheat and rye.

During the 20th century, large food companies began to sell more packaged foods. Many of these companies were based in Western nations, but they sold their goods all over the world.

Serving a meal that was already prepared and packaged in a bag, can, or box saved time. People no longer had to buy a variety of fresh foods and then cook them to create a meal.

Health watch

Sweet, fatty, and salty foods

Humans have a tendency to favor sweet, salty, and fatty foods. Tens of thousands of years ago, sweetness told humans that a fruit was ripe and good to eat. These humans were drawn to fatty foods because the foods held many calories, which they needed in case food supplies became scarce. Some fat is also essential for good health, as is sodium, the mineral that is the source of table salt. The desire for sweet, fatty, and salty foods helped humans survive.

People still have these desires, but in the modern industrialized world, realities have changed. Sweets often provide empty calories, meaning they do not supply nutrients the body needs. A shortage of calories is not a problem and, as a result, people often eat more unhealthy types of fat than they need. And people get far more salt than they need in processed foods.

The processed foods, however, tended to be high in sugar, salt, and fat. Sugar and vegetable oils are cheap ingredients, thanks to government subsidies—and so affordable products at supermarkets became full of them. And food companies responded to the fact that consumers like sweet, fatty, and salty foods.

What do you think?

Is it right for governments to pay farmers to raise some crops, so prices will be low—even if eating too much of some of these foods is not the best option for our health? Would it be good for governments to place special taxes on certain unhealthy foods, so that people will not buy them as frequently?

Thanks to these developments throughout the 20th century, the Western diet of today usually includes refined grains, large amounts of sugar, fat from both plants and animals, and fewer fresh fruits and vegetables than people ate even a decade or so ago. The Western diet also tends to be low in fiber, a part of some foods that helps improve digestive health and lowers blood pressure.

Replacing traditional diets

The spread of the Western diet has led to some traditional diets being replaced, often with negative consequences for health. For example, in 2011 the small Pacific island of Nauru was announced to be the fattest nation in the world. Phosphate mining in the country has led to more money being available for food and the islanders have chosen to spend it on a Western diet – their favorite meal is fried chicken! The Japanese historically have low cholesterol levels because their diet includes a lot of fish, but more recently levels have risen to match those in western Europe. This is largely a result of some Japanese having adopted a Western diet.

A typical fast-food meal of burgers, fries, and a soft drink often contains as much as half the fat a 12-year-old should eat during an entire day.

Cows, sacred to many Indians, roam the streets of Delhi.

Vegetarianism and veganism

While the Western diet is popular, it is not the only option people choose. For a variety of reasons, some people choose not to eat some or all animal products. Religion can play a part, as certain faiths do not allow the eating of certain foods. Hindus, for example, do not eat beef, and Jews and Muslims do not eat pork.

Vegetarianism around the world

The number of vegetarians around the world is small. A 2008 survey showed that just over seven million Americans called themselves vegetarians, while about three times as many were **pescatarians**. In Europe, the United Kingdom has the most vegetarians, according to a 2006 poll. About 3.6 million people, or 6 percent of the population, called themselves vegetarians. India, the home of several religions that promote vegetarianism, has the world's largest vegetarian population. A 2006 survey there found that 399 million people—or 40 percent of the country—did not eat meat of any kind.

On a wider scale, **vegetarians** do not eat any kind of animal flesh. They might choose to do this because their religion prohibits the killing of any creature. Other vegetarians think the raising of cattle and other livestock is bad for the environment (see pages 32 to 35). The amount of water, land, and energy it takes to raise livestock is rising, as the demand for meat increases. Other vegetarians believe avoiding animal products is healthier for them.

Most vegetarians will eat eggs and dairy products. They are called ovo (egg) and lacto (milk) vegetarians. Some people consider themselves vegetarians yet still eat fish. They call themselves pescatarians, from "*pesce*," the Italian word for fish.

One step beyond vegetarianism is **veganism**. Vegans will not eat any animal products (including eggs and milk) or wear clothing produced from animal leather or fur. Vegans also approach their diet for a number of reasons, including religious and environmental ones. But most vegans believe it is cruel to keep animals as food sources, even if they are not killed. In some cases, vegans cannot get all the nutrients they need from their diet. Doctors sometimes recommend that they take pills containing vitamin B_{12} to make sure they get enough of it.

Health watch

Vegetarianism and health

Eating a vegetarian diet can be healthy, but it depends on the choices each person makes. A meal with lots of cheese and fried foods could be meatless—but it could still have too much fat and too many calories. Vegetarians also have to make sure they get enough protein from sources that are not heavy in calories and fat, as some dairy products can be.

Beans, especially soybeans, can provide some of that needed protein. But not all soy products are necessarily healthy, either. Many "fake" meats made from soy are highly processed, meaning they have added ingredients, including salt. And oils added to some of these products increase their fat content. Soy meats and other soy products made from non-organic soybeans might pose another health risk. The beans are processed with the chemical hexane. The hexane separates the fat and protein in the raw beans. In the air, hexane is considered a harmful pollutant. No one knows if the amount used to process non-organic soy is dangerous.

Conscientious omnivores

Many people choose vegetarianism and related diets because they think it is better for the planet. But a growing number of people believe they can help the planet while still eating meat. They are known as conscientious omnivores, a term coined by Australian professor Peter Singer. "Conscientious" means paying attention to what is right and wrong, and trying to do what is right. "Omnivore" describes animals, such as humans, that can eat both meat and plant products.

Meats, fish, and dairy products often travel long distances in airplanes or trucks before they reach a family's kitchen. Transporting those foods releases gases that contribute to global warming (see box below). Conscientious omnivores want to avoid causing this damage.

No one set of rules or beliefs defines conscientious omnivores. But in general, they prefer to eat food grown locally. Many only eat meat raised on small farms they have visited, so they know the animals were treated well before they were killed. This treatment usually includes feeding the animals grass, which is better for them than the grain used on most large farms. Smaller farms also tend to use fewer chemicals to raise their livestock— chemicals that conscientious omnivores want to avoid eating in their meat or adding to the environment.

Environment watch

Global warming

Scientists have measured an increase in the average temperature on Earth over the last 200 years, a trend called global warming. Historically, the planet has seen long-term temperatures rise and fall, but most scientists believe the recent increase is tied to human activity—specifically, the release of so-called **greenhouse gases**. These gases collect in the atmosphere and trap heat close to Earth. The burning of **fossil fuels**—for example, gasoline in cars—releases greenhouse gases. As we will see, many greenhouse gases also result from growing crops and raising cattle (see pages 32 to 39).

Many scientists believe the warming trend will continue as more of these gases are produced. And rising temperatures could create many problems, from severe droughts in some regions to heavier rainfall in others. These changes could then have a harmful effect on agriculture.

Another recent trend in diets is known as the **slow food** movement. The movement began in 1986, when Carlo Petrini protested the opening of a McDonald's restaurant in Rome, Italy. Petrini was rebelling against the idea of "fast" food—of people eating on the run and away from their homes and families.

Petrini wants people to connect to their food and to connect to other people through food. He believes that taking time to choose fresh, local ingredients, then cooking them at home, helps people appreciate the higher quality of those foods. Sharing a home-cooked meal with others gives diners a chance to truly enjoy the taste—and each other's company.

Today, more than 100,000 people in dozens of countries support Petrini's movement and its goals. Chief among these goals is eating food that is "clean," meaning

Health watch

A benefit of meat

Despite the health dangers of eating too much fatty meat, many scientists still see meat as part of a healthy diet. That might be even more true in **developing countries**, where traditional diets are low in meat.

A two-year study done in Kenya several years ago showed that children given a small amount of beef each day did better in school than children who received only milk or no other extra protein. The kids given meat also developed more muscles in their arms. The study, however, focused on children from poor, rural areas. The British Dietetic Association believed the results would probably be different among children in Western nations, where protein is more readily available from a variety of sources.

When cows feed on grass, which is much healthier for the animals than the grain they are fed at factory farms, they provide far healthier meat and milk to humans.

that producing it does not hurt the environment. With crops, that means reducing the use of chemical **fertilizers**. For livestock, it means buying grass-fed beef. For both, it means buying locally whenever possible. And the production of the food should be fair, meaning farmworkers should make a decent wage. The whole process creates a system in which food is raised and prepared in the best way for the planet and for people.

Case study:
The battle over food labeling

Sometimes consumers, governments, and food companies do not agree on how food products should be labeled. For example, a new food labeling system was proposed in the EU that would have used a system of coding that looked like traffic lights on food packaging to indicate if foods contained high levels of sugar, salt, and fat. A red light would mean a food should only be eaten occasionally, because it was high in one or more of those ingredients, while a green light meant the food was generally healthy.

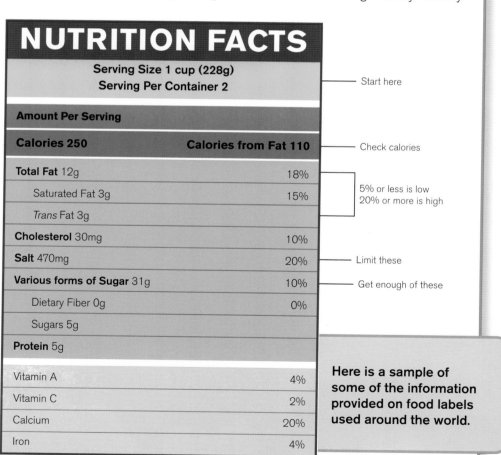

NUTRITION FACTS

Serving Size 1 cup (228g)
Serving Per Container 2

Start here

Amount Per Serving

Calories 250	Calories from Fat 110

Check calories

Total Fat 12g	18%
Saturated Fat 3g	15%
Trans Fat 3g	
Cholesterol 30mg	10%
Salt 470mg	20%
Various forms of Sugar 31g	10%
Dietary Fiber 0g	0%
Sugars 5g	
Protein 5g	

5% or less is low
20% or more is high

Limit these

Get enough of these

Vitamin A	4%
Vitamin C	2%
Calcium	20%
Iron	4%

Here is a sample of some of the information provided on food labels used around the world.

Carlo Petrini was a food and wine writer before he began Slow Food International to promote good, clean, and fair food for everyone.

Given the different choices people make about their diets, knowing exactly what is in their foods is important. In Western countries, governments set rules for how foods are labeled. The labels include a food's ingredients, nutritional information, and, at times, details on how the food was prepared or processed.

Some countries also have strict definitions for foods labeled organic, which means grown without chemicals. In the United States and European Union (EU), for example, an organic food product must have at least 95 percent organic ingredients. Also, farms must be certified as organic. This means that farmers must prove they do not use chemicals and that their fields have been chemical-free for several years.

Some European food companies spent about $1.5 billion on ads and information to stop the new labeling system. They feared that consumers would stop buying products labeled with a red light—which is exactly what health officials wanted. The officials hoped to convince people not to eat foods that could lead to medical problems.

The labeling system was not introduced, but EU lawmakers did make some changes to food labels. All meat, poultry, and dairy products now have to show where the food was produced. This lets consumers buy local products, if they prefer. Also certain ingredients, including artificial sweeteners and a kind of harmful fat called trans fat, now have to be listed. This labeling battle showed how government, business, and other groups shape what kind of information consumers get to help them make their food choices.

From Farm to Table

Modern agriculture and technology give you many food choices. Food can come from around the world or from a farm across town. What you choose to put on your plate affects companies and people from all levels of the food system.

Unless you grow your own food, what you eat comes originally from a farm or the world's waters. People raise crops and livestock and catch fish (although some fish is farmed as well). Most of the food is processed in some way—raw crops become ingredients for a packaged meal, or cattle or hogs are butchered into cuts of meat. Then the products are brought to the stores, where you and other consumers purchase it.

When you buy goods in your local grocery store, you are perhaps unaware of the concerns of the people who produce the food. Instead you are focused on buying the best food you can at prices you and your family can afford. You know they can choose from thousands of items to suit any diet. But your decisions go far beyond your own table and the local store.

Unseen dangers

Seeing the packaged goods on shelves, people might not realize that agriculture is one of the most dangerous professions in the world. Figures from the U.S. Bureau of Labor Statistics usually show that in the United States, agriculture and commercial fishing have a high number of work-related deaths compared to other industries. That was the case in 2008, when farmers and ranchers had 324 work-related deaths, second only to truck drivers. Internationally, figures show that agriculture is the third-most dangerous job, after mining and construction, based on the number of work-related accidents and illnesses. Deaths and illness in agriculture often involve equipment accidents and exposure to harmful chemicals.

Given that accidents can occur long before a food is packaged and sold, consumers might not know if workers on a certain farm or in a certain plant face more dangerous conditions than the law allows. But news reports often highlight bad conditions at certain companies. If consumers believe the conditions are wrong and the companies could do more to ensure worker safety, they have a choice. They can choose not to buy products from that company.

But knowing whether a company generally treats its workers well is not always easy to know. It might require Internet research or joining organizations that track corporate practices. Many consumers feel that they do not have the time or energy to track the activities of the many companies that make their food.

Processing chicken is hard, potentially dangerous work.

Unseen poverty

While not all agricultural jobs are dangerous, many are difficult. In many places, workers put in long days for little pay and often plant and pick crops by hand. In some cases, wages are so low that these workers cannot afford to buy food.

With the growth of industrialized farming, it is increasingly common that only massive agribusiness corporations have the money needed to invest in equipment, chemicals, and large areas of land. This means that many small farmers have gone out of business because they cannot compete. Many of them end up working for the larger companies at low wages—lower than what they made when they worked for themselves.

Blood on the meat

Meatpackers face some of the most dangerous working conditions in the world. The U.S. meatpacking industry is centered in the Midwest. Many of the workers are immigrants who do not speak English well and fear they could lose their jobs if they complain about conditions or report accidents.

Records show that accidents do occur. A 2009 poll of several hundred workers in Nebraska plants found 62 percent had recently suffered injuries. Most common were repetitive-motion injuries. Cuts were also common, as workers stand close together and must work quickly to prepare hundreds of cattle per day. Even cleaners at the plants face risks, as they can accidentally turn on machines that can maim or kill.

The effects of fish

The choice to buy fish can have an effect on people far from where you live. Demand for fish is rising worldwide, as more people see it as a healthy source of protein. Fishing fleets in developing countries, especially in Asia, send their fish to Western markets, where they can make more money than at home. But sending the fish overseas reduces the supply at home, raising the price for the local consumers. So, buying only local fish could mean more affordable fish for someone on the other side of the globe.

In addition, some fleets from Western nations fish the waters off of developing nations. Combined with the local fishers, they deplete the supply of fish. The killing off of fish species, or greatly reducing their numbers, can have a negative impact on the local ocean environment. Killing off species can also end fishing as a career for local residents.

These boats are part of Thailand's commercial fishing fleet, which catches such fish as tuna, swordfish, and mahi mahi.

Workers also face problems where chickens are processed. Brazil is now a world leader in raising and processing chickens, which are shipped around the world. As they prepare the birds, many workers—mostly women—suffer injuries from performing the same repetitive motions over and over. Few companies offer workers any health insurance that will pay to treat these injuries.

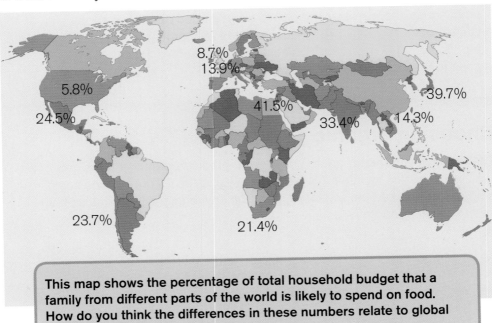

This map shows the percentage of total household budget that a family from different parts of the world is likely to spend on food. How do you think the differences in these numbers relate to global food production?

Case study:
Bananas

In 2004 the Food and Agriculture Organization of the United Nations (FAO) looked at the mass production of bananas. For every dollar spent on bananas, the workers who picked them earned about two cents. Unlike foods such as grains, bananas need little processing, so the profits are not going toward processing costs—rather, almost all of it goes to the companies, not the workers.

Choosing organic

The decision whether or not to buy organic products greatly affects how food gets from its source to you. Buying organic, locally grown food could help reduce the number of chemicals in the environment. It could also help keep a local farmer in business.

But, as we have seen, in most cases the cost of organic products is higher, as farmers usually run smaller operations than agribusinesses do. The larger farms can save money by using more expensive equipment that performs certain tasks quickly. They also rely on chemicals to control weeds and pests. The methods for doing those chores on organic farms often require more human labor, which raises a farmer's expenses.

Organic sales

Still, many people are willing to pay extra for organic products. Into the first years of the 21st century, the sale of organic foods rose in many Western nations. Germany, for example, saw the sales rise 14 percent in 2007 and 10 percent in 2008. The United Kingdom saw sales rise an average of 16 percent each year between 2003 and 2008, and in the United States, annual sales rose from $1 billion in 1990 to almost $25 billion in 2009.

The rise in the sale of organic foods came as more supermarkets carried them. Wal-Mart and stores it owns, for example, began adding more organic foods (see page 28). And some grocery stores featured a wide variety of organic goods, such as the Whole Foods chain in the United States. But, as with organic goods sold elsewhere, prices were higher than for conventional foods.

Questions about buying organic

Then, in 2008 the world entered a deep recession—an economic downturn that causes people to lose jobs and spend less money. Some people began to question whether it was worth paying the extra price for organic food. Fueling that question were several government reports. A 2010 report from the U.S. Department of Agriculture found that organic eggs are no healthier than ones produced under factory conditions. Another report from the United Kingdom said organic foods are not more nutritious than foods grown with chemicals.

And in some cases, organic methods did not end the problems some people associate with factory farms. In the United Kingdom, a 2007 study found eggs and chicken were sometimes sold as organic, even though the chickens that laid them were in crowded sheds with no light, and even though the birds themselves did not eat organic food. The large companies that used these practices were not technically breaking the law at that time. But they were not following the standards most consumers assumed all organic producers followed.

Case study:
Wal-Mart and the demands of consumers

Retailers sell the goods consumers demand. For example, if no one wanted pork chops or kiwi fruit, stores would not sell them. As the world's largest retailer, Wal-Mart keeps track of what consumers want to eat. If it sees people buying organic goods at other stores, it adds more organic products at its stores—which sell food throughout the United States and in many different countries as well, including the United Kingdom, Brazil, and Japan.

Because of its size, Wal-Mart has great influence on the price of goods. It expects its suppliers to provide items at the lowest cost possible. Due to the demand Wal-Mart creates, farmers will produce as much as they can of what Wal-Mart wants. In the early 2000s, Wal-Mart began selling organic milk, and it quickly sold more of it than any other U.S. grocery company. Its demand for the milk meant that dairy farmers had a guaranteed customer for their product.

Wal-Mart also started a program it called Heritage Agriculture, an effort to support locally grown crops. The goal is to find produce grown just a day's drive or less from its warehouses. Wal-Mart will sell this produce at nearby stores, rather than trucking in fruits and vegetables from much farther away. Usually, food grown organically or on small local farms can be more expensive than conventional food. Wal-Mart saves money in transportation costs and by working directly with the farmers, instead of going through "middlemen" who add to the price for their own profit.

Over the years, Wal-Mart has often been criticized for its practices. Workers have sued the company over some issues, including forcing employees to work extra hours without pay. The company has been found guilty several times and paid hundreds of millions of dollars in fines. And the company's low prices can drive much smaller stores out of business. But in terms of food, some of Wal-Mart's new efforts are winning praise. U.S. **environmentalist** Michelle Harvey said in 2010, "It's getting harder and harder to hate Wal-Mart."

Going local

Whether people buy organic or not, they have many choices about where they buy their food. Large supermarkets get most of the sales. But a growing number of people are turning to farmers' markets and local ranches to buy produce and meat.

Some are part of the slow food movement, which stresses connecting people to the sources of their food. The group calls consumers "co-producers." It believes that when people get to know farmers, their jobs, and their problems, the consumers take a more active role in food production. Their knowledge of where and how food is produced also stirs their interest in and enjoyment of cooking and eating their meals.

Some people who choose to buy locally are called **locavores**. Often they try to eat only food grown within a certain distance of their homes—perhaps 160 kilometers (100 miles). Locavores list a number of benefits to buying locally as much as possible. For one, the food is fresher. For another, the money spent on food stays in the local community, rather than going to large corporations that might be based thousands of miles away. And eating food that has not traveled far cuts down on "**food miles**" (see page 38).

Community-supported agriculture

One way to buy local produce is to join a **community-supported agriculture (CSA)** farm. Most CSA farms are small, organic operations. Members of a CSA pay a set amount of money at the beginning of the growing season. Farmers sell a certain number of shares, based on how much they think they can produce. As crops are harvested, the members receive a share of what is ripe that week.

For farmers, the CSA system means they know before they start planting that they will sell all their crops. And if the weather is bad, they will still have income. Members know they take a risk that the harvest might be less than expected—though in good years, it can be more. Some CSA members also volunteer on the farms, helping the farmers save some expenses—and giving themselves good exercise in the fresh air.

Limits of buying locally

Buying locally, however, can limit which foods you eat at certain times of the year. For example, in many areas, fresh, local tomatoes are only available for a few months each year. The same is true of many other vegetables and fruits. And certain regions do not have the climate to grow some crops at all. Bananas and other tropical fruits, for example, will not grow in northern Europe. Because of these realities, locavores have to limit their diet in some ways to stick to their "buy local" beliefs.

The Marylebone Farmer's Market is one of more than a dozen serving London, England.

And a CSA has limits, too. If all that is harvested one week is turnips and beets, and members do not like them, they are stuck. All they get that week is turnips and beets. Yet for many people, eating only locally grown foods is a challenge they think is enjoyable and worthwhile.

Case study:
Farming in the city

How can people in the heart of a city get easy access to fresh, locally grown produce? Detroit, Michigan, has one answer. The city has long been the center of the U.S. auto industry. But over the past few decades, the car companies based there have cut thousands of jobs. The area has lost many residents, and many who remain struggle with poverty.

To provide affordable, locally grown produce, several groups set up the Garden Resource Program to help local residents grow their own food. The city's bad economy has left behind vacant lots where homes and businesses once stood. These lots are now home to hundreds of urban farms. Some farms raise just a few crops, while a few urban farmers raise pigs or keep honeybees. One nonprofit group wants to build organic farms. The farms would be part of new neighborhoods that also include schools and housing.

Even larger is the dream of multimillionaire John Hantz. The Detroit resident wants to invest $30 million to create the world's largest urban farm. Hantz says the farm will provide jobs and locally grown food for restaurants and stores, as well as use "green" technology that does not hurt the environment. He plans to start with 28 hectares (70 acres) of vacant land and then grow from there.

As you can see, there is not just one route for food to get from its source to you. Each method has plusses and minuses for the consumer and the environment. What you buy reflects what is important to you.

A Detroit resident harvests tomatoes in one of that city's many urban farms, located next to an abandoned building.

Food and the Environment

As you've seen, producing and consuming food affects people and events far beyond the farm or the family dining table. Some of the food industry's greatest impact is on the environment—water, air, and other life forms on the planet. Here are some examples—and the ways your choices can increase or improve environmental problems.

The rising popularity of meat

For more and more people around the world, meat is an important source of protein. Meat production has tripled over the past 30 years and is expected to keep rising. One explanation is that people in developing nations, such as China, have more money to spend on food, and they increasingly choose to buy meat (see chart).

Meat consumption in China	
Year	Kilograms (pounds) per person
1995	25 (55)
1999	31 (68)
2000	50 (110)
2008	53 (117)

With the increase in meat production (and the raising of chickens for eggs and cows for milk), the world now has more than 1.7 billion livestock animals. The farms and ranches that raise these animals cover more than 25 percent of the land on Earth.

Some meat, like some produce, is grown sustainably. The farmers try to limit the impact raising livestock has on the environment. And some consumers look for locally raised meat, dairy, and eggs for the same reason others choose to buy produce at farmers' markets. The food is fresher and money stays in the local community.

But on a global scale, factory farming of livestock is rising, especially in developing nations. This industrialized production of meat, dairy, and eggs has a large impact on the environment.

Raising livestock requires much more water than is needed to grow grains for consumers. Compared to growing a pound of rice, a pound of beef requires almost twice as much water. That includes drinking water for the cow, the water used to grow its feed (commonly corn and soy), water used in waste removal on farms, and other uses.

Yet the amount of water available on Earth has natural limits—and adds to the environmental cost of meat. Only about 2.5 percent of the world's water supply is freshwater, and much of that is in the form of ice and snow that never melt. Some parts of the world already face severe water shortages. In other areas, groundwater is being used quickly, making it harder and more expensive to bring it to the surface. Many people worry that this precious resource is being increasingly used up for meat, a food product that is perhaps not necessary in such large amounts in people's diets.

China is the world leader in hog production and consumes the most pork.

Livestock, pollution, and global warming

Another connection between livestock and water is pollution. On large farms, livestock waste is stored in large tanks called lagoons. At times, some of the waste leaks from the tanks and enters nearby waterways. Farmers also use **manure** as a fertilizer, but once on the fields some can run off into nearby bodies of water.

On a typical U.S. hog farm such as this one, the pigs are raised in the white buildings shown here, while their manure is collected in the lagoon behind them.

In some cases, harmful chemicals from the manure can travel from rivers into large bodies of water.

If manure is left in the lagoons found on factory farms, it releases the gas methane, which is a greenhouse gas that causes global warming (see page 18). Livestock themselves also add to global warming. Cows, as they digest food, release methane. Some critics therefore argue that people should eat less meat and consume fewer dairy products, as this would reduce the number of cattle raised—and would begin to reduce their contribution to global warming.

Possible solutions

There are other solutions as well. For example, some farms are trying to capture methane and use it as a fuel source. To counteract the damage cattle cause to the environment, farmers around the world are also exploring ways to use plant and animal waste (known as **biomass**) to create power. One example of biomass being used for power is illustrated by a farm in China which raises about 250,000 cows. The gas produced from the manure of the farm's cattle is being used to create electricity. Each year, the farm should be able to meet the electricity needs of as many as 15,000 people, while reducing the production of carbon dioxide, a greenhouse gas produced when fossil fuels are used to create electricity.

The Chinese project and other sources of biomass energy will not run out, as petroleum some day will, and they also release fewer harmful gases. These and other solutions (see box at right) will help create a balance between the desire many people have to eat meat and the health of the environment.

Environment watch

Fuel of the future?

Given the hazards of animal manure, scientists have been looking for safer ways to get rid of it—and perhaps replace some fossil fuels at the same time. In Illinois, scientists created a method for heating pig manure, putting it under high pressure, and producing a fuel. Manure from cattle can be treated the same way. The method is not perfect, as the fuel produced is not as clean as fuel from petroleum. But Tom Bruno, a scientist who studied the method, thinks it can be improved to produce cleaner fuel. On average, the manure produced from a pig before it is slaughtered for its meat would produce about 79 liters (21 gallons) of fuel.

Concern over crops

While industrialized and factory farming of meat raises many environmental issues, growing crops presents its own problems. Just as chemicals from animal manure can leak into bodies of water, so can the chemicals from factory-made fertilizers used in agriculture.

One chemical from fertilizers in particular—nitrogen—can create what scientists call dead zones, areas where no sea life can survive. The Gulf of Mexico has one of the world's worst dead zones. Tons of nitrogen from animal waste reach the Gulf, as rain carries it from farms along the Mississippi River. (Nitrogen also enters water from manure, although agricultural nitrogen is a bigger problem.)

A researcher in Thailand inspects genetically modified papaya.

Some scientists fear that the chemical runoff from fertilizers could have other harmful effects, as more of it reaches the world's waterways. Phosphorous, another of the main components of fertilizer, promotes the growth of certain aquatic life. In Belize, in Central America, scientists have noticed larger mosquito populations in areas where the chemical has spurred plant growth in water. These mosquitoes have the tendency to carry diseases such as malaria. In other studies, scientists saw an increase in other harmful **organisms** in areas where nitrogen and phosphorous collect in water.

Genetically modified organisms

One possible way to reduce the use of fertilizer and other agricultural chemicals is by growing **genetically modified organisms**, often called GMOs. All living organisms have genes, which contain chemicals that determine their traits. The genes are passed on from one generation to the next. In nature small changes in genes occur over time. But in the lab, scientists add new genetic material to create a quick and specific change to an organism's traits. In farming, scientists have created new crops that resist disease and pests or can grow under extreme weather conditions, such as drought. This reduces the need for fertilizers.

GMOs, however, have stirred their own controversy. Some scientists and food organizations argue that not enough study has been done on the potential dangers of GMOs to humans, animals, and the environment. Critics of GMOs say the world's largest food producer, the United States, has not properly studied the potential damages.

GMO lawsuits

Several lawsuits have been filed in the United States challenging the use of GMO crops. In one case, farmers feared their organic alfalfa crops could be contaminated by GMO alfalfa. Seeds can be blown from one farm to another, and bees can carry the pollen from a genetically modified plant to an organic farm some distance away. In another challenge, the Center for Food Safety argued that the U.S. government had not done enough to study the possible damage caused by modified sugar beets.

U.S. courts so far have given mixed messages on the issue of GMOs in agriculture. In 2010 the U.S. Supreme Court, the highest court in the country, decided the modified alfalfa could be grown. Yet a lower court that year ordered a halt to growing the sugar beets until the government did more research on their possible effects.

Agriculture and global warming

Most of the greenhouse gases created in agriculture come from fertilizers. Chemicals in fertilizers react with the soil and the air to create nitrous oxide, a greenhouse gas, which then rises into the atmosphere.

> "We've used more fertilizer in the last 20 years than in all of human history."
> —Scientist Alan Townsend, University of Colorado

As we have seen, the burning of fuels called fossil fuels is another big contributor to global warming (see page 18). Farms of all sizes burn fossil fuels to run trucks and tractors. This produces greenhouse gases, especially carbon dioxide. Fossil fuels are also burned to create electricity. The use is highest in countries that rely on petroleum, natural gas, and coal to power their electric generators.

Food miles

Cars and trucks also burn fossil fuels when they transport foods like meats, fish, and dairy products long distances before they reach a family's kitchen. Those distances create what are called food miles. Simply put, this is the distance food travels from where it is raised until it reaches your home.

Shipping food over long distances is not something new. Several thousand years ago, traders brought spices across Asia. But the spices were not a large part of most people's daily diet. Today, many common foods routinely travel thousands of miles to reach billions of people.

The winding path from farm to table

The distance from farm to table is not a straight line—food travels to various stops along the way, as it is processed, warehoused, and finally brought to a store. In the 1990s, a report from the United Kingdom showed that the average distance food traveled had increased by 60 percent over the previous decades. A 1998 U.S. study showed that in that country, six types of vegetables traveled, on average, more than 3,200 kilometers (2,000 miles) to reach a major market in Chicago, a city located roughly in the middle of the country. Only two items—mushrooms and pumpkins—traveled fewer than 800 kilometers (500 miles).

In particular, meat production creates more food miles compared to raising crops. By the time a serving of beef arrives at a table, farmers and processors have used 16 times as many fossil fuels as it would take to bring the same calories of vegetables to a consumer. So, many people argue that avoiding meat, fish, and dairy avoid these food miles altogether. Alternately, buying products from local farmers is a way of drastically reducing food miles.

Food miles required to prepare a meal of pasta with sauce in London		
Food item	Grown/made in	Food miles (approximately)
Pasta	Italy	900
Dried tomatoes	Italy	1,000
Olive oil	Italy	1,000
Salt	English coast	40
Pepper	India	4,700
		Total food miles=7,640

Some food companies have stopped shipping their products in trucks like these and now use trains and boats that produce fewer greenhouse gases.

Difficult choices

The issue of food miles has fueled the locavore movement (see page 29). But at the same time, some consumers want to eat organic foods, but they cannot find them from local sources. Some food experts, such as Michael Pollan, say it is probably better for the environment to buy local conventional food, rather than organic food from thousands of miles away.

What would you do?

Would you give up one of your favorite foods if it came from a farm far from your home? What distance would be too far for you to eat it?

GARETH EDWARD-JONES

Looking more closely at food miles

Welsh scientist Gareth Edward-Jones says focusing too much on food miles is not the best measure of the energy used to produce—and eat—food. He has studied the systems that bring certain foods from farms to consumers, trying to measure the **carbon footprint** created along the way. This "footprint" refers to the total amount of greenhouse gases created by any system, such as the food system, over a given period.

So, the carbon footprint of a particular food includes the energy used to produce and process it, as well as to transport it. Soils themselves also release gases, and this amount varies from one type of soil to another. Grasslands, for example, have a smaller carbon footprint than paddies, where rice is grown. Even the energy used to cook the food adds to its total footprint. Edward-Jones says that it takes almost as much energy to boil a potato as it does to raise a potato in the United Kingdom and transport it to a home.

Edward-Jones's research has led him to believe that people sometimes put too much importance on food miles, without looking at the larger picture. He says, "My personal advice would be to do whatever best satisfies your conscience, but don't kid yourself that by so doing you are saving the world."

Soybeans are seen here growing through leftover stalks of wheat, in an example of no-till farming.

At times, though, a crop grown in another country could be better for the environment than one grown locally. For example, in parts of Spain, the climate is warm enough to grow tomatoes year-round. Less energy is used to ship the tomatoes from Spain to the United Kingdom than is used to grow tomatoes in the United Kingdom in greenhouses.

Less work, fewer gases

Farmers have another way to try to reduce greenhouse gases, particularly carbon dioxide. Some use a practice called **no-till farming**. On typical farms, machines till, or stir up, the soil before planting. Tilling releases carbon dioxide into the air. With no-till farming, however, farmers do not turn over the soil before each new crop. Instead, special machines shoot the seeds into the ground, through the leftover plants from the last harvest and the surface of the ground.

This planting method reduces erosion—the process of water carrying away soil and its nutrients. No-till farming also adds nutrients naturally, thanks to the decay of the leftover plants. And farmers save time and money preparing their fields this way. But no-till is not perfect, as it still requires the use of herbicides (chemicals that kill weeds) and so is not suited for organic farming.

Clearly, choosing food to have the least impact on the planet requires gathering facts. Concerned consumers have to do research, knowing that many questions about the "best" food to eat do not have easy answers.

Healthy Choices

When people shop for food, they weigh many factors, such as what they can afford, what is easy to prepare, and what they like. For some people, health is also a factor—they want to choose food that is low in fat or other substances that can harm the body. Or, on the other hand, they want foods high in the vitamins and minerals thought to help fight off disease.

While considering all these different things, more people are also thinking about the ethics of their choices. How are the foods produced, and do the methods harm the environment? How are livestock treated in the production of meat, dairy, and eggs? Can the foods they eat be both good for them and good for the planet?

Finding the right fat

Foods have three main nutrients—fats, proteins, and carbohydrates. The body needs all three to survive, as well as small amounts of other substances called micronutrients.

There are four major fat types, and some are better for your health than others. From healthiest to least healthy, these types are monounsaturated, polyunsaturated, saturated, and trans fats. Fat helps cells develop and aid in absorbing other nutrients. Fat also helps keep the body warm. But the modern Western diet is often high in fat, and too much dietary fat is linked to higher risks of **obesity**, various cancers, and other illnesses. Those risks have made the consumption of fat one of the major health issues of the 21st century.

People need to eat lower-fat diets for the good of their health. But they can also do so for the good of the world at large. For example, palm oil is a source of saturated fat, which is considered among the worst of the four main types of fat. Palm oil is raised in countries where rain forests are often cleared to grow the trees that are the source of palm oil. If more people chose not to buy the oil or foods that contained it, the demand would fall, and rain forests would not be cut down.

A better choice for the body—and the environment—is olive oil, which is high in monounsaturated fat. Raising olives also has less of an impact on the environment, compared to producing palm oil. In this way, people can make healthy choices that help both their bodies and the planet.

Olive oil, one of the healthiest fats, is shown here being bottled in a modern factory.

Animal products

Experts have different opinions about the value of animal products such as meat, dairy products, and eggs in people's diets. It is known, however, that the right amounts of these foods can provide necessary proteins. In the wrong amounts, they can add unhealthy saturated fat.

As we have seen (see pages 16 and 17), vegetarians and vegans have strong opinions about the ethical issues of eating animal products. But most people who eat meat or fish do not see an ethical problem with killing animals for food. They might have religious beliefs that say God created animals and Earth for humans to use. Or perhaps they never really considered if it is right or wrong—they just know that people have eaten meat for thousands of years, it provides nutrients, and it tastes good.

At least one thinker has argued that animals benefitted from the process of being domesticated (tamed by humans). Thousands of years ago, wild cattle and sheep learned that human communities offered them protection from wild animals and provided a regular supply of food. Individual sheep or cattle might be killed for food by humans, but the species as a whole thrived once it was domesticated.

Concerns

Today, however, a growing number of people are concerned about the problems associated with the factory farming of livestock—both ethical and health-related problems. The methods used to raise livestock at large factories are designed to produce fat in the animals as quickly and cheaply as possible. That means cramming chickens, cattle, and hogs into tight spaces, so as many as possible can be raised on one farm.

Factory farms also overuse drugs to boost the animals' growth and prevent sickness. In particular, millions of tons of **antibiotics** are given to livestock each year. Antibiotics kill **bacteria** that cause disease. But over time, some bacteria develop resistance to the antibiotics—the drugs no longer kill them. These bacteria could then leave the farm—either through the food or through the environment. The most frightening danger comes if the bacteria make people sick. If this happens and the bacteria have become resistant to common forms of antibiotics, doctors might not be able to treat the disease the bacteria cause.

Health watch

Back to the past

Should modern people look to the earliest humans for clues about what to eat? That is what followers of the paleo diet say. "Paleo" is short for "Paleolithic," which is the scientific name for the Stone Age—when early humans had only stones and animal bones for tools. That era was also before the rise of agriculture, so people relied on hunting animals and gathering nuts, berries, and wild plants for food.

U.S. professor Loren Cordain is one of the biggest supporters of the paleo diet, which calls for eating lean (less fatty) meats, seafood, and fruits and vegetables. The diet eliminates most or all grains, sugar, salt, dairy products, and beans—foods associated with agriculture. Cordain and some other people believe that those foods have led to an increase in many illnesses, particularly heart disease and obesity. Some modern paleo eaters also avoid mass-produced food as much as they can. That can mean eating meat from wild animals or animals raised on grass rather than grain. Those choices would help reduce the demand for factory-farmed meat and the chemicals it introduces to the environment.

Finding a balance

Is there a way to balance ethics and eating meat? Conscientious omnivores (see pages 18 and 19) say their food choice helps everyone. They look for meat that has been raised under the most humane conditions possible. This means the animals are allowed to roam freely, instead of being kept in cages. They are fed their natural diets, not corn or grains that are filled with chemicals. The animals live pain-free, and the farmers strive to kill them as quickly and painlessly as possible.

These farming conditions also produce leaner meat, meaning less saturated fat in the consumer's diet. Plus, livestock that are fed grass—their natural diet—instead of grains will produce meat, dairy, and eggs with more of the helpful components of fat, particularly omega-3 fatty acids, which have been shown to lower the risk of heart disease. But on the downside, conscientiously produced meat is more expensive than meat from factory farms. Choosing the healthier method of production can be a tough economic choice for families with low incomes.

More than half of the world's fish-farming takes place in Asia, where fish is a main source of protein.

Issues with fish

In the push for healthier eating, fish is often mentioned as a healthy option. Most fish is lower in saturated fat than meat, and some varieties, such as salmon, mackerel, and sardines, are high in omega-3 fatty acids.

But ethical eating means more than just choosing a particular kind of fish. The source of the fish plays a role. Some fishers and environmentalists promote sustainable fishing. But with so many varieties of fish eaten around the world, there is no one rule for knowing how to choose the most sustainable and healthy fish. Some species of fish caught in the wild are in danger of being overfished—they are being caught faster than they can reproduce to keep their populations stable.

Today, the world's fishers catch more than twice as much fish as is being replaced, making most wild fishing unsustainable.

Aquaculture involves raising fish and shellfish under controlled conditions—for example, salmon farming. But aquaculture presents its own issues. Raising salmon, a "heart-healthy" fish, means catching a lot of wild fish to feed the farmed ones. And waste from the salmon pens can enter nearby waters, harming the wildlife. The best fish farms grow species that do not feed on other fish and are located in areas where wider environmental damage is limited.

JAMIE OLIVER

Eating—and doing—the right thing

Fans of good food around the world know British celebrity chef Jamie Oliver (pictured below). As the popularity of his cookbooks and cooking programs grew, Oliver decided to do something good for society. He filmed a show in the United Kingdom, *Jamie's School Dinners*, that illustrated how bad some school food was—and how much better it could be. Oliver's goal was for schools to provide good-tasting, healthy foods that kids would want to eat.

His efforts led the British government to create the School Food Trust and spend more money across the country on nutritious school meals. The trust also educates students about the role food plays in local communities and overall sustainability.

In his other efforts, Oliver has stressed teaching kids how to cook and has focused on using locally grown, seasonal crops, which reduce food miles. Calling for a "food revolution" in the United States, he asked Americans to demand that school lunches feature "naked" ingredients—such as fresh fruits and vegetables—and fewer processed foods.

Food-borne illnesses

Knowing how food is produced can help you make better choices for yourself and the planet. But some dangers in food are hidden—such as food-borne illnesses. Scientists have identified several major sources of food-borne illnesses. Perhaps the best known are *E. coli* , Listeria, and salmonella. According to the World Health Organization, in Western nations up to 30 percent of the population each year suffers some kind of illness from food. Most cases are not severe, but people have died from eating tainted food.

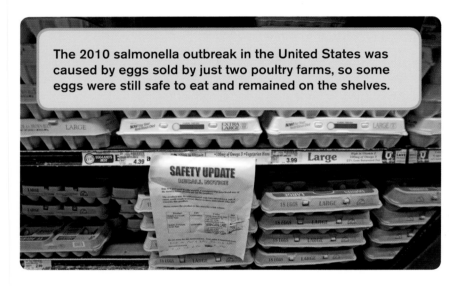

The 2010 salmonella outbreak in the United States was caused by eggs sold by just two poultry farms, so some eggs were still safe to eat and remained on the shelves.

Top ten countries for reported cases of salmonella in 2008	
Country	Cases of salmonella per 100,000 people
Slovakia	134.27
Czech Republic	105.55
Lithuania	94.07
San Marino	83.41
Croatia	83.17
Hungary	71.39
Denmark	66.57
Finland	58.89
Slovenia	52.37
Estonia	48.26

Farms large and small can produce food that contains the germs that cause disease. Meat, dairy, and eggs are most likely to cause disease, but crops have been the source of several major outbreaks of *E. coli*. With livestock, some of the disease-causing organisms live on or inside the animals. With raw foods, such as vegetables, some harmful organisms reach the crops through runoff water from meat and dairy farms.

Lowering the risks

Farmers take steps to prevent the spread of food-borne illnesses. In dairy farming, for example, milk goes through a heating process called pasteurization, which kills most harmful organisms. Many other foods go through a process called irradiation. Radiation is a form of energy that can kill organisms of all kinds. Radiation, though, is very harmful in large doses, which has led some people to oppose food irradiation. Many international health groups, however, have backed the safety of irradiated foods.

Despite the measures to keep food safe, food-borne illnesses still occur. Beef presents several particular health concerns. The ground beef sold in many grocery stores might come from several different countries, let alone different farms. Because of this process, a contaminated cow's meat could be spread far beyond its source.

In 2010 the United States had a major outbreak of salmonella traced to eggs that came from factory farms. About 1,400 people became sick, and more than 500 million eggs already in stores were pulled off shelves to prevent further illness.

Dangers like these explain why some people prefer locally raised foods—they know exactly where this food comes from. They may even be able to visit the farm to talk to the farmer about potential problems. Buying packaged meat or eggs in supermarkets makes this impossible.

The right thing to do

As you have read, the food system is both global and local, small and large. It offers great variety and affordable food for many people—but not all. And the variety and low prices found in Western nations can have other costs. Different farming and food production practices pose risks to human health and the environment. Consumers have to decide for themselves what are the most ethical choices for them when they buy their food. With knowledge, they can do what best fits their values.

Food Issues: Security and Sustainability

Climate challenges

According to the Food and Agriculture Organization of the United Nations (FAO), changes to the climate present a huge challenge to food security (see page 9). The problem is especially difficult in developing countries that already struggle to meet all their food needs. These countries face two problems—they must produce more food to feed growing populations, but climate change will make it harder to grow more food. Some proposed solutions include using more animal manure for fertilizer, and practicing conservation agriculture (CA). This can involve using no-till farming or planting crops that put nitrogen into the soil. For aquaculture, one way to reduce carbon gases is by raising sea vegetables and shellfish, which require less energy to raise than most fish.

The need for nutrition	
This chart shows the percentage of people who were undernourished—a sign of food insecurity—in various parts of the world between 2005-2007.	
Region	Percent undernourished
Developing countries	16
Asia and the Pacific	16
Latin America and Caribbean	8
Near East and North Africa	7
Sub-Saharan Africa	28

Food from Mother Earth

Every two years, food producers from six continents travel from their home countries and meet in Torino, Italy to attend the Terra Madre Conference ("Terra Madre" translates to "Mother Earth"). This conference on sustainable agriculture was created by Carlo Petrini, founder of the Slow Food movement (see pages 19 and 20). Farmers, fishers, ranchers, beekeepers, and others involved in helping to feed people attend the conference to discuss new trends in agriculture.

The 2010 event attracted more than 6,000 people. Some of the topics included were biodiversity; energy issues, such as reducing reliance on oil in food production and other areas; and the effects of subsidies on food choices. The Terra Madre Conference brings attention to the choices consumers can make to address some of these issues. For instance, consumers can choose to buy food raised without the use of fossil fuels, or they can choose a wide variety of fruits, vegetables, and grains to promote crop diversity.

"My people's ancestors were farmers, and we have grown up as farmers. We have inherited crop varieties and we have a responsibility to pass it on to the next generation. In this life, if we keep food in our hands our future will be secure."
—Malebo Mancho Maze, a member of the Gamo ethnic group of Ethiopia and Terra Madre participant

"You can simply stop participating in a system that abuses animals or poisons the water or squanders jet fuel flying asparagus around the world. You can vote with your fork, in other words, and you can do it three times a day."
—Michael Pollan, food writer and researcher

Glossary

agribusiness company involved in the large-scale raising and production of food

agriculture raising of crops and animals for food

antibiotics chemicals that kill small organisms called bacteria

aquaculture raising of fish and shellfish under controlled conditions

bacteria small organisms that live inside larger life forms, water, soil, and air; some bacteria cause diseases

biomass source of energy that comes from plants and animal waste

carbon footprint total amount of carbon produced by a certain process or action

community-supported agriculture (CSA) small, usually organic farms that sell shares of the crops they produce

consumer person who buys goods

developing country nation that is building industries and creating more wealth but that is still poorer than the wealthiest nations

diabetes disease marked by the body's inability to produce or properly use the natural chemical insulin

drought long period without rain in a particular region

environmentalist person who makes an effort to protect the environment from dangers created by humans

ethical relating to good behavior that does not harm others

factory farm operation that uses machinery to raise a large amount of livestock or crops

fertilizer chemical that help crops grow

food miles total distance a food product or its ingredients travel to go from the farm to the place where it's eaten

food security concept of everyone having easy access to affordable, nutritious food

fossil fuel fuel, such as coal and petroleum, that was created hundreds of millions of years ago from the remains of organisms

genetically modified organism (GMO) animal or plant that has chemicals inside it, called genes, changed to give it new traits

global warming slow increase in temperatures recorded around the world

greenhouse gas gas that collects above Earth and traps in heat, adding to global warming

industrialized featuring the widespread use of machines and technology to produce a variety of goods

locavore person who tries to eat only food grown locally

manure animal waste used as fertilizer

no-till farming method of preparing soil that does not turn the remains of the last year's crop back into the ground

nutrient chemicals in foods that are essential for life

obesity condition marked by a high percentage of body fat, which can lead to life-threatening diseases

organic farming method that does not use chemicals to raise crops

organism living creature

pescatarian person who is mostly vegetarian but still eats fish

pollution chemicals that are harmful to the environment

process turn a raw crop or animal into a food product

protein chemical found in certain foods that humans need to live

refine remove part of a grain to prepare it for use in food

slow food approach to food production and consumption that stresses eating local, sustainable food and enjoying meals with friends and family

sovereignty freedom to run one's own affairs

subsidy money given to farmers by a government for raising certain agricultural products

sustainable able to be kept going or producing in a healthy way

urban relating to a city

veganism practice of not eating or using any products that came from animals

vegetarian person who does not eat any kind of meat or fish

Further Information

Books

Baines, John D. *Food and Farming* (*Global Village* series). Mankato, MN: Smart Apple Media, 2009.

Ballard, Carol. *Food For Feeling Healthy* (*Making Healthy Food Choices* series). Chicago, IL: Heinemann Library, 2007.

Chevat, Richie, and Michael Pollan. *The Omnivore's Dilemma: The Secrets Behind What You Eat*. New York, NY: Dial, 2009.

Kukathas, Uma, ed. *The Global Food Crisis* (*Current Controversies* series). Detroit, MI: Greenhaven, 2009.

Mason, Paul. *Food* (*Planet Under Pressure* series). Chicago, IL: Heinemann Library, 2006.

Redlin, Janice L. *Land Abuse and Soil Erosion* (*Understanding Global Issues* series). New York, NY: Weigl, 2007.

Spilsbury, Richard, and Louise Spilsbury. *From Farm to Table* (*Food and Farming* series). New York, NY: PowerKids, 2011.

Websites

www.fao.org
The website of the Food and Agriculture Organization of the United Nations looks at food security and hunger from a global perspective, with statistics on food production from around the world.

www.sustainabletable.org
The Sustainable Table website was created by a group dedicated to sustainable agriculture. The site includes useful tips on where to find sustainable products.

www.usda.gov
The official U.S. Department of Agriculture site has the latest news on farming in the United States, a history of U.S. agriculture, and information on such topics as soils and food safety.

www.cgfi.org
The Center for Global Food Issues is a U.S.-based organization that examines food issues, focusing on the role of business and free trade, rather than laws and government rules, to solve food problems.

www.foodsecurity.org
Focused on North America, the Community Food Security Coalition promotes locally raised, sustainable agriculture as well as a food system dedicated to justice and democracy.

www.slowfood.com
The official website of the Slow Food International movement founded by Carlo Petrini has a listing of events and educational resources about food.

Topics for further research

What are the main agricultural products raised in your country or region? Use the Internet to locate a government agency involved with agriculture to find out. Is most of the food eaten locally or shipped elsewhere? Could you buy more of the food that is grown locally and cut down on similar products you currently buy that travel long distances?

Identify local groups that promote food sustainability. What are their specific methods and goals?

Does your school have any kind of program to reduce the amount of food wasted? Is there information provided to students on the nutritional information of food served at your school?

Index